A Scarlet Thread
In a Sober Skein

Nithila K Shankar
Illustrated by Sasha Maran

Copyright © 2025 by Nithila K Shankar

All rights reserved.

No part of this publication may be reproduced, distributed, or transmitted in any form or by any means, including photocopying, recording, or other electronic or mechanical methods, without the prior written permission of the publisher, except as permitted by India copyright law.
First edition 2025

For my parents, who have always given me their love and support
And my sister, who helped me publish this book
And my best friend, who has inspired me in so many ways.

Table of Contents

Preface

I have been writing poetry since the third grade; drawn to its ability to capture the emotions we struggle to name. *A Scarlet Thread in a Sober Skein* is a reflection of that fascination—an exploration of the way deep feeling intertwines with the fabric of everyday life.

This collection speaks of love, loss, longing, and hope—the raw, universal currents beneath our composed exteriors. The scarlet thread represents those moments of intensity, weaving through the sober skein of reason and restraint. I hope these poems resonate with you, stir something familiar, and remind you that emotion, in all its shades, is what makes us human.

—Nithila K Shankar

I'm nobody, who are you?
Are you nobody too?

Fleur-de-Lis

The wood that succors a spindly tree
Is far less kind to fleur-de-lis
Where the green and brown grow wild and free,
Is there place for pink and white to be?

But it springs forth nonetheless
A slip a joy in wilderness
In a field of powder-green watercress,
Is a crimson rose any the less?

Those who different will feel the pain
Of being a scarlet thread in a sober skein
Of being treated like a burden, a bane
Because, because they are not the same

Bread and Roses

I want life and a reason to live

I want enough to eat and enough to give

I want to sing and lend others my voice

I want to be happy and watch others rejoice

I want fire to cook and fire for light

I want to sleep and ensure others sleep the night

I want sustenance and beauty true

I want bread and roses too

I Have Not Time

I have not time to sit and stare
As dragonflies fill the morning air
No time to watch the sky turn blue
And watch the day bloom anew

I have not time to laugh & sing
As I wonder what the day will bring.
No time to see the spring burst into flower
And not notice each and every ticking hour

I have not time to slumber sound
To bury all worry beneath the ground.
No time to be silent and still awhile
To let my thoughts settle, let myself smile.

I have no time, no time to lose
To quiet, as chaos stops & peace ensues
No time to breathe softly and close my eyes
And let my dreams fill up the dusky skies

She, Emilie

Once there was a girl who lived atop a banyan tree
She had fiery red locks, wild and free
Blazing baby blues that'd see through a lie
Kind to a fault, but one to defy

Laughter like sunflowers, a snarky sweet smile
She flipped her hair, and laughed at every trial
Truly she was allowed to do anything she liked
Which is how everyday she swam and hiked

Climbed and fell, did every errand the townsfolk sent
Ran through the brush to her heart's content
No one could hold back the light-footed child
Not even her kind neighbors she so easily beguiled

One day, when the winds were strong and the currents rough
She climbed the cliff to Blind Man's Bluff
And she felt invincible as she laughed into the roaring sky

The waves crashed below, a violent lullaby

They found her body, blue with cold
She too proud to do as told
She, fiery in her passion, gentle in her kindness
She who made her village sigh with every ripped dress

She, Emilie, for whom the whole world wept

Sensory Overload

Colours blur together
As sky flips to ground
Noises bleed together
An overwhelming sound

A faint realization
Drowned out by waves of fears
Blood tastes like metal
And sad, salty tears

Soft and hard
Flesh and things not alive
Pressing against skin
Pain flowing from inside

Shouts of panic
People crowding around
Overcome once more
Sinking in a sea of evils abound

I can't see
I can't hear
I can't think
All I feel is fear

The Little Spark

Once upon a time, there was a little spark
That glowed like an ember in the blue-black dark
She was young and kind and brave and true
But alas! The little spark was foolish too

For all her kindness, for all her wit
The little spark was careless and cared not a bit
for the words of her mother, so old & wise
She laughed in the face of her worried cries

Her mother warned her not to go near the water
For she truly loved her exasperating daughter
But this only excited the stubborn spark
Who crept off in the night, into the starlit dark

She slipped off to the House her mother spoke about
Her pounding heart betrayed nary a doubt
She peered into a puddle in front of a box

Balanced precariously atop a pile of rocks

In it, she saw herself, a bright little spark
Glowing like an ember in the blue-black dark
Her face was young & kind & brave & true
But alas! She could not see that she was foolish too

Suddenly, the dog gave an almighty bark
Scaring the wits out of the poor little spark
She tripped & she flailed, heart fear-wrought
Cursing the adventure she'd foolishly sought

The night was quiet, the night was dark
For 'twas the end of the poor little spark

*'If the world is your oyster
Then the ocean of the galaxy
must surely belong to me'*

The Blind Boy

I talk of all the things I see,
I say the sky burns blue
But how on Earth is he
To know that it is true?

I say the leaves are em'rald green
And the bark is brown as earth
But how can he know unless he's seen
Leaves dancing in their boundless mirth

I tell him the wild beauty
Of the feral golden flames
But he'll ever hear nor see
Naught but their names

I tell him that the dawn is red
But does he know what red is?
Most likely everything I said
Drowned in that blurry, black abyss

I once asked him out of curiosity
For I bore him no animosity
"What do you think colors are?"
And he replied, his eyes star

"Silver's the color of my mother's hair
The color of love, beautiful and rare
Brown's the color of my father's eyes
Of endless patience and endless sighs"

But sometimes I think
I am more blind than me
Because I am oft fooled
By what I can see

I see a kind, beguiling face
But he sees the undertone of lies
Those truths I cannot trace
He finds before he tries

He may be suspended
In endless black
But his effortless clarity
Is something I envy and lack

Health

Health is like a treasure you hold in your hand
Open your fingers, it'll slip through like sand
It whispers in silence, a gentle refrain,
Through strong beating hearts and unbroken veins.

Nourish it well with the fruit of the earth,
The air, the water, the sunshine's mirth.
Move with intent, let your body be free,
A temple of strength, the words of Bruce Lee.

Cherished with care, it blossoms and grows,
Neglected, it fades, as the weary soul knows.
Maintaining it well is life's greatest test
A beautiful balance twixt vigour and rest

Health is a promise, a chance to explore,
Mountains, rivers, oceans and more.
So guard it with wisdom, let your eyes shine bright
For health is the flame that keeps life alight

Ballerina

Her toes touch the earth

Where no spotlight gleams

Chasing rhythms lost

In forgotten dreams

The fields stretch wide

Her prison is of air

Each twirl a rebellion

An escape from despair

Her hands reach skywards

But tethered she must stay

Bound to a world

That cares not for ballet

She could leap through the heavens

She could defy the stars

Yet she still dances here

With worn shoes and rusty bars

Oh, let her go
To where she belongs
So she can dance for the world
And to the most vibrant songs

Here she dips and sways
For the cows and the cat
How could you lock up a girl
Who can dance like that?

And for someone so caged
And yet so free
She deserves to live
Life's symphony

Her soul cries out,
A whispered plea
"Don't let my freedom
Die with me"

From the top of her head
To the littlest toe
Flows forth a talent
The world should know

Oh, farmer, old farmer
Open the gate
Let your little girl twirl
Let her tempt fate

Without her you shall live
But do not deny her this
A life unlived
And a stage she'll miss

True Beauty

Beauty's bloom is a fleeting sight,
A fragile flower that's bathed in light.
A canvas painted in shades soft and fair,
A moment captured, beyond compare.

A youthful glow, a radiant face,
A graceful form, a perfect grace.
But time's relentless hand will steal,
Everything that, to us, feels real

Clear lines will fade, smooth skin will sag,
The quickest feet shall begin to lag.
Yet, true beauty, deep and pure,
Endures forever, that's for sure.

It's in the heart, the light of the soul,
A gentle kindness, should be our goal
A love that's selfless, pure and true,
A beauty lasting, ever new.

Beyond the surface, where beauty resides,
A deeper essence, where truth abides.

It's in the kindness, the compassion shown,
The empathy felt, so deeply known.

It's in the laughter, the joy, the boundless mirth,
The spirit that soars, of assured self-worth.
It's in the resilience, the strength within,
The courage to face life's every whim.

So let us cherish, this fleeting grace,
The beauty that shines on every face.
For true beauty, transcends the passing years,
A timeless treasure that ever endears.

Songbird

I heard a songbird singing high in a tree
It sounds like a melody meant for me
Sweeping notes that tell of my life
Of all the joys and all the strife

The highs of happiness and soaring joy
All the things I love and enjoy
The depths of despair and boiling rage
Crashing to an awful life I could not exchange

Then the trembling notes of guilt, of pain
The bane I'd fed others, horrors I cannot contain
The jagged song of unspeakable sorrow
The souls I'd doomed to never see the morrow

I feel sick of what I'd done
'Neath the tree, 'fore the setting sun
As that little bird flew away
I felt half glad, but half wished it'd stay

I know not how long I stood transfixed
Listening, learning as I stayed betwixt
The grass behind and rocks ahead
One painful and unknown, the other painted red

All I know is when I went to sleep.
I had no dreams of dangers deep
But slept with peace upon my brow
Thinking of naught but the here and now.

Of the songbird with the enchanted voice.
The creature who believed, who gave me a choice
So I repented and did all I could've.
To repay for what I'd cost, for what I should've

I was not a killer, nor was I a criminal
I was not a bally, but I was a coward
I watched and listened in silence
And that is what I did

I did not hurt
But I let them hurt
They did not come for me
So I did not protest

But no more shall I quiet my voice for
I shall shout and scream of those who cannot
I shall not tell of what happens
And become a songbird myself

Her Lament

They said, 'Go home,'

'You'll be safe there.'

But,

He screams at me, beats me (till I'm gasping for air)

Is that what you call safety?

I don't feel safe

They said, 'Work,'

'At least you'll have financial freedom.'

But,

They want things I'll never give, so I'll never get ahead (it's
a man's

kingdom)

Is that what you call freedom?

I don't feel free

They said, 'Go out,'

'Have fun, don't worry, you don't need a knife up your
sleeve.

But,

They leer at me on the streets, call after me (I'm not that

-naive)

Is that what you call fun?

I don't feel like I'm having fun

They said, 'Get help,'

'Find someone you trust, to turn to when things are dire.'

But,

They don't listen, think I'm looking for attention (I'm no liar)

Is that what you call help?

I don't feel helped

They ask 'Why are you so paranoid?'

'No one's going to jump out of your shadow'

But,

(How would you know?)

They say, 'You reap what you sow.'

They say, 'It's your fault,'

'Just look how you dress,

How you act, leading him on, no less!'

'You should've been careful.'

(How is this on me?!)

But,

I say, 'It's not my fault,

I should be able to dress how I like,

Act like myself, speak to who I like’

‘I shouldn’t have to be careful.”

IT'S NOT MY FAULT

Little Pearl

A little girl curls up to take a nap
On her mother's gingham lap
Her hair is stroked by calloused hands
That worked their life in callous lands

Her voice is hoarse and hoarse with song
But when she speaks, her voice is strong
"They say no man is born in chains
But the blood of slaves run through our veins"

"If I must suffer, so let it be
So that you might live a better life than me
My will is as strong as the next woman who sings
Of skin as dark as a raven's wings."

"I wish you joy where I've known pain,
A path unmarked by blood or bane.
May your feet walk on the earth so free,
A future bright where you can be"

Slowly, quickly, a hand unfurls
Trembling, shaking, amongst cinnamon curls
If the world was her oyster, her baby was the pearl
She prays for the world to be kind to her girl

I am, I am, I am

I am a sword
Forged in the flames of adversity
I am strong
Because I refused to break

I am bamboo
Watered with my own tears
I do not fall
Because I sway with the wind

I am silk
Woven tightly by those unworthy of me
I do not tear
Because I do not let myself fall apart

I am a nightshade
Beautiful and deadly
I smile in public and seethe in private
Because I know looks can deceive

I am a rose
In bloom, covered with thorns
I prick those who try to uproot me

Because I learned to shield myself from others

I am fire
Dancing with rage
I burn all those who touch me
Because I know anger is the best way to prevent hurt

The Piper Calls

The Piper comes over the fields yonder
What is the here for? Nervous souls ponder
O'er the crest of the Eternal mountain
Through the valleys, through the glen.

He pipes a merry tune, a haunting tune
Of blood & war & tears & ruin.
He pipes a merry tune, a haunting tune
Of teary eyes, of smiles, of a promise, 'soon'

A song that heals & hurts and makes you smile & scream
A song that makes you despair & hope & anguish & dream
It makes you cover your ears and beg for it to go away
But it also makes you harder listen, and wish that it would
stay

He pipes the sons of the country to the battlegrounds
Enticing them with his pleasing Siren-sounds
Over the fields and rivers and lakes and seas
Past hundreds and thousands of rustling trees.

Their mothers and sisters beam with pride
But cry when the sequester themselves a side

Those young boys and not-so-young men in uniform
Fresh, bright, thinking themselves ready for the steam

Living and dying for the motherland
Proud faces, tilted chins, fists form on each trembling hand.
The Piper pipes and so on we must march.
In this glorious walk of doom, towards the shining arch

Till he stops and lets us catch our breath
We must trip along in this dance of death.
The dip and sway of the music exhilarates
The notes of which all of us knows & loves & hates

The Piper's gait quickens as he turns not one
Time to see if we follow; He skips on, his back to the sun
His shadows twist and turn, gnarly, till they are the stuff of
nightmares. Unfazed equally by praise and smiles of curses
and glares.

The wicked piper will then disappear round the bend
Leaving us all disoriented and confused in the end
With a scattered, world be split world behind us reeling
A deep green poison deep inside preventing it from healing

World War One has come and gone.
Twenty Years, and life goes on
Those who lived have still war-torn eyes
That can't forget their fellows' cries.

The havoc the wicked piper wrought

Felt even by those who haven't fought
Ghastly, horrid just like me
Who took a man's eyes but still can see.

In the back of my mind, a haunting melody.
Will forever play, rising, falling with no remedy.
How I wish, I wish he'd let us all be.
But the Piper has left a mark, that sets my family apart
from me

The Piper pipes for his unwitting thrall
As nations rise and nations fall
Let this be a warning to us all
Never heed the Piper's call

Strong

A white, white rose with
A green, green stem
Prickly thorns, stabbing
Those who hold them
A white knuckled hand
That grips too tight
Bloody fingers illuminated

In the moon's waning light
Crimson stains mercilessly
The pure, flawless white
Tears fall, finally
In the dead of night
From silver orbs that tried
So hard to be strong
That have felt far too much
For far too long

A solitary figure bows
Over the unforgiving flower
Lonely, quiet, too silent
During the witching hour
The only reprieve

Twixt the taxing days
Are the moon-lit nights
And what 'ver the garden says.

Blood washed away by
Desperate, painful tears
Shoulders shaking silently
Revealing agonizing fears
As the first rays
Of the rising bun peek out
Bright and teasing
They peer about

The figure gracefully rises
From the muddy ground
Stone-faced, jaw set
Making not a single sound
Blood is wiped
Hands are bound
The mask is perfect
Swirling all around.

Sweet and perfect
Kind but distant
Strong but delicate
Pretty and pleasant
Walking back home, to
Whatever life has in store
Walking back to hell, to
Be strong once more

Spirits Call

Though I may be gone, do not weep
As I did sow, so shall I reap
I will cross the golden gates
Past the whispering, weaving fates

Think not that I have left you behind
In years to come, I shall come to mind
And you will ascend, as I now do
With a mind so clear and purpose true

Though I may have passed, do not grieve
I will be with you still, morn and eve
I will watch over you forevermore
Till you grow wings, then you will soar

Though I may have left, I won't be far
I'll come, when you wish upon a falling star
When you smile and laugh and frown and cry,
I will stay though I say goodbye

Though I may be gone, do not despair
I linger still, in the very air
Though I may leave, you must stay
Till you too decide, to come away.

Once again, in a time to come
When your soul is free & your body numb
In a realm beyond that of men
(I know not when) we shall meet again.

When We Were Young

When we were young, we had genuine smiles
We ran together in groups instead of walking in files.
When we told our stories, we were met with interest & pride
We could play pretend & clutch toys to our side

Our eyes were untempered by misery or loss
We'd dream of shawls of starlight and dresses of moss
The world was so simple, we never told lies
We were invincible, so we said casual goodbyes.

We were always so happy, right down to our bones
Hopping round barefoot, cursing sharp stones
We saw fortunes in fires and stories in seas
We laid in the grass and spoke the language of trees

Our fingers were stained with purple & pink
We drank from little paper cups right out of the sink
Our mothers sighed & picked wood chips out of hair
We laughed unashamedly, till we were gasping of air

We turned somersaults & cartwheels in even the sand
Banging pots & pans together made us a band
We scrambled around looking for dandelions & clover
Held hands solemnly and promised 'best friends forever'

Cracked Walls

Cracks run deep
In these water-stained walls
Grief laid the foundation-
But faith built these halls

Trust shingled the
Red sunbaked roof
Windows clear with belief
And strengthened with proof

But what can we do,
If trust is broken?
If faith is betrayed,
And belief a mere token?

What can we do,
If we're just puppets and dolls?
If we're the reason
That this great house falls?

What can we do
To fix what is shattered?
How can we bandage
That which is battered?

The burden is heavy
And its wholly undue
Why should all of us suffer
For the sake of a few?

So, what can we do?

Bring long estranged sons
Back into the fold
Let the disdained daughters
Feel the love of old

A long cracking house
Cannot be healed in a day
But we will mend the cracks
And we will stay

And is that not all we can ask for?
That all of us stay?

Tower of Lies

The rain grew heavy with every stride
The rich man cowered in his castle of pride
He hid away from the rage, the cries
His tower tilted, his tower of lies

The peasants gather round, anger clear in their eyes
As they demand the rich man answer their blood-curdling cries
They storm the gates and drag him to his knees
Ignoring his groveling and terrified pleas

For the rich man was hated, the rich man was cruel
He feasted in peacocks and fed his people gruel
And he was a man driven by hedonistic greed
Who lived off the poor, like so many of his creed

His tower was built with a thousand blood-stained bricks
While his people live in homes of sticks
The rich man cowered, no longer brave
As he sobbed on the floor like a common slave

There is a flash of silver on rainy blue skies
As beautiful and deadly as the rich man's lies
And the blue is now red, but the silver is bright
Like the souls of the liberated that fateful night

The Edge of Slumber

Between the realms of dawn's embrace
And the yawning expanse of deep blue space
A liminal space, a silken thread,
Where dreams and waking thoughts are bred.

The body sleeps, yet the mind does stir,
A distant whisper, a vaguest blur,
Of rustling leaves, a bird's soft tune,
A symphony of shadows that swirl and swoon.

The finest line 'twixt wake and sleep
Is where we find ourselves in dangers deep
Yet the blade of joy will cut it through
As every dream gives way to you

The room, a canvas, bathed in gray,
Where shapes emerge, then fall away,
A fleeting glimpse, a phantom hand,
A dream's reflection, soft, yet grand.

The air is still, yet there's a gentle sigh,
As time itself seems to freeze in place and then drift by,
A moment held, suspended, free,
In this sweet realm of reverie.

And in this space, where worlds collide,
New thoughts are born, where dreams reside,
A tapestry of fleeting grace,
A beauty in this liminal space.

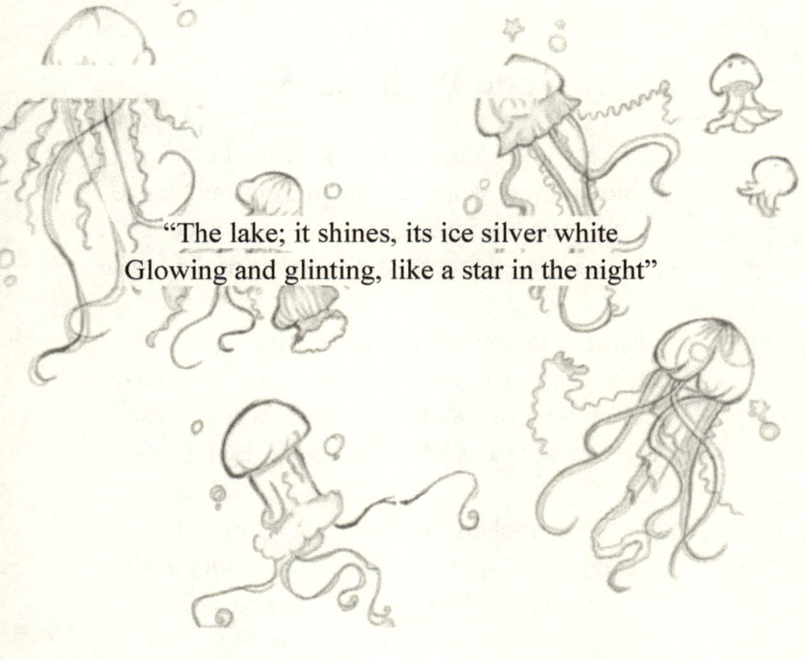

"The lake; it shines, its ice silver white
Glowing and glinting, like a star in the night"

Gone With the Wind

A whispering song sung by the trees
Is blown away gently by the murmuring breeze
A humming tune crooned by the bees
Is blown away gently by the soft sigh of the breeze

Ripples in the water made by fish with ease
But even more easily blown away by the breeze
The sand forms dunes but dunes won't freeze
They are ever so gently blown away by the breeze

Every spoken word you cannot rescind
For every word spoken will be gone with the wind
Don't you know all you do and say
Will be blown away, by the wind someday

Crimson

A storm within, a tempest in the soul,
A righteous rage that I don't want to control.
A crimson tide erupts swift and blinding,
Fury at the cruel, the callous, and unminding

The world moves on, unaware of my plight
As I drown in the red that encompasses my sight
They only know my words are like a weapon
A brightest beacon that no one can reckon

Two trembling fists, a voice that resounds
I will forge ahead, breaking new grounds
It has no place in our world, the cruelty of the past
Yet the wrongs of our folk will last and they'll last

Every word, every gesture, is fuel to my fire,
But instead of understanding, they only admire
The quiet in my silence, the calm in my rage,
Telling me I'm mad, like I'm locked in a cage.

My anger's not silly, not a child's little tantrum
I'm just trying to solve a grownup's conundrum
On TV, grown men shout over the tiniest trifles
At least I'm not picking up grenades or rifles

Our world will stand still, we won't ever evolve
If children are told to sit still and not get involved
You tell me anger is weakness, it's not good to get upset
If that's true, then humanity needs a hard reset

But anger's not weakness, it's just a fight to be heard,
Yet they see us as fragile, just souls that're disturbed.
We're not broken, just tired, of the weight that we must bear,
Of the faults of our parents, that we children must repair

Her Resilience

In halls of steel and boardrooms bright,
Where deals are struck with forceful might,
She sits, a whisper in the roar,
A different cadence at her core.

They speak of sports and weekend brews,
Of locker room jokes and coded clues,
A language forged in many a boyhood game
Must be hard for that unlucky dame.

When she speaks up, she goes unheard,
A million voices drown out every word
If she shouts too loud, they say she's difficult
There is no winning with them; it's so typical

They stride with confidence so bold,
Their tales in the past are told,
Of fathers' firms and legacies grand,
She holds a different story in her hand.

She offers thoughts, precise and keen,
But her brilliance remains unseen,
They prefer the utterances of their own,
A rhythmic beat they've always known.

She longs to bridge the widening gap,
So she can forget she ain't a chap
To find a space where she can rest
From feeling like an unwelcome guest.

Yet in her heart, a fire burns,
A quiet strength that slowly learns,
To navigate this foreign land,
And carve a space where she can stand.

For though the culture may exclude her
She has endured far stormier weather,
She will grow and flourish, strong and tall,
And break the mold, and conquer all.

Chains of Memory

A little girl curls up to take a nap
On her mother's gingham lap
Her hair is stroked by calloused hands
That worked their life in callous lands

Her voice is hoarse and hoarse with song
But when she speaks, her voice is strong
"They say no man is born in chains
But the blood of slaves run through our veins"

"If I must suffer, so let it be
So that you might live a better life than me
My will is as strong as the next woman who sings
Of skin as dark as a raven's wings."

"I wish you joy where I've known pain,
A path unmarked by blood or bane.
May your feet walk on the earth so free,
A future bright where you can be"

Slowly, quickly, a hand unfurls
Trembling, shaking, amongst cinnamon curls
If the world was her oyster, her baby was the pearl
She prays for the world to be kind to her girl

A Few Words

Each poem in this book is a testament to the art of language, crafted with care and infused with meaning. As you turn these pages, allow yourself to pause, reflect, and feel.Step in, savor its beauty, and let the verses speak to you. Each piece echoes the ache of longing and offers a glimpse into the poet, Nithila's heart and, in turn, our own.

Dipti SV
Program Manager, Walmart India

This book unlocks the mind as if it is a journey through explosive thoughts. Nithila employs soft, subtle, and eloquent language, akin to that produced by an instrument. It is as though her mind is being unlocked, her thoughts exploding like fireworks in the night sky. She possesses a kindred spirit with the ability to unlock the minds of others through her words.

- Janani Ramachandran
M.A., M.Phil English ;PGT ENGLISH

Nithila excels in everything she does and is a great reader herself! She is a true inspiration to her other cousins and friends! Books are her best friend and I'm so glad she is publishing a poetry book! Looking forward to enjoying the read!

-Nithya Natarajan
Auditor Senior Manager

Acknowledgements

This book would not have been possible without the love, support, and encouragement of some truly incredible people.

To my parents and grandparents—thank you for your unwavering belief in me. Your love, wisdom, and constant encouragement have shaped me in more ways than I can express. This journey has been as much yours as it has been mine.

To my sister, Krithika—my editor, my sounding board, and my fiercest supporter. Your keen eye and honest feedback have helped shape this book into what it is today. I couldn't have asked for a better person to walk this path with me.

To my talented illustrators, Sasha Maran and Sahana Viswanathan—your artistry has brought my words to life in ways I never could have imagined. Your creativity and dedication have made this book all the more special, and I am deeply grateful.

To my best friend, Prisha Nitin—thank you for inspiring me in countless ways. Your encouragement, laughter, and wisdom have been a guiding light through this journey. I am endlessly grateful for your friendship and for always pushing me to be my best.

To my wonderful beta readers, Subashini Bala, Harini Krishnan, Sahana Viswanathan and Aruna Jayalakshmi—your insights and thoughtful feedback have been invaluable. Thank you for taking the time to read, reflect, and help me refine this story. Your support means the world to me.

This book is a reflection of all the love, kindness, and brilliance I have been lucky enough to be surrounded by. Thank you all for being a part of this journey with me.

With gratitude,

-Nithila K S

About the Author

Nithila K Shankar is a sixteen-year-old poet whose work delves into themes of nature and human's emotions. She has won several poetry competitions, like the Chennai Poetry Slam. She has also developed and hosted a book drive to donate books to orphanages so that every child can realize the beauty of words. Since a young age she has been an avid reader of fictional books and started to write poetry in third grade. She has also won ten gold distinction medals in the International English Olympiad (including zonal and international levels). Her favorite authors are Rick Riordan, Madeleine L'Engle, L.M.Montgomery and Madeline Miller.

Nithila lives in Coimbatore and continues to write and share her poetry with the world.

www.ingramcontent.com/pod-product-compliance
Lightning Source LLC
Chambersburg PA
CBHW022115150726
47990CB00003B/1356